This Book Belongs To:

 _____

Tips For Creating Passwords

✔️ **Make it memorable.** Do you have a favorite song, poem, or quote? Here's how to turn it into a password:

Quote: "A rose by any other name would smell as sweet." – William Shakespeare

Now let's take the first letter of each word and randomly capitalize, then add the author's initials and the year it became important to the user.

Password: aRbaoNWsasWs12

✔️ **Memorize part of the password - don't write it down.** Log the other part of the password in this book.

Here's how that works: The ocean is very important to me, so I am going to use the word 'ocean' for the part I memorize. If someone finds my written password, they won't be able to use it to gain access to my accounts because it is only part of the real password.

So in my head is **ocean** and written in this book is the random second part of the password : **tlmHpS*09**

The full password becomes: **oceantlmHpS*09**

This way, you can use one word over and over by adding it to different letters, characters and numbers for each account.

TOP TIP: Combine both of the tips above!

A Website Name

Website URL

Username 👤

Password 🔒

Password Hint

 Notes

Website Name

Website URL

Username 👤

Password 🔒

Password Hint

Notes

Special Instructions

Website Name

Website URL

Username 👤

Password 🔒

Password Hint

Notes

Website Name

Website URL

Username 👤

Password 🔒

Password Hint

Notes

Special Instructions

A

Website Name

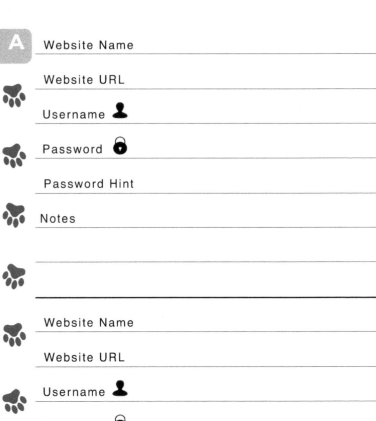

Website URL

Username

Password

Password Hint

Notes

Website Name

Website URL

Username

Password

Password Hint

Notes

Special Instructions

Website Name

Website URL

Username 👤

Password 🔒

Password Hint

Notes

Website Name

Website URL

Username 👤

Password 🔒

Password Hint

Notes

Special Instructions

B Website Name

Website URL

Username

Password 🔒

Password Hint

Notes

Website Name

Website URL

Username

Password 🔒

Password Hint

Notes

Special Instructions

Website Name

Website URL

Username 👤

Password 🔒

Password Hint

Notes

Website Name

Website URL

Username 👤

Password 🔒

Password Hint

Notes

Special Instructions

B Website Name

 Website URL

Username

 Password

Password Hint

 Notes

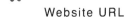

Website Name

Website URL

Username

Password

Password Hint

Notes

Special Instructions

Website Name

Website URL

Username 👤

Password 🔒

Password Hint

Notes

Website Name

Website URL

Username 👤

Password 🔒

Password Hint

Notes

Special Instructions

C Website Name

Website URL

Username 👤

Password 🔒

Password Hint

Notes

Website Name

Website URL

Username 👤

Password 🔒

Password Hint

Notes

Special Instructions

Website Name

Website URL

Username 👤

Password 🔒

Password Hint

Notes

Website Name

Website URL

Username 👤

Password 🔒

Password Hint

Notes

Special Instructions

C

Website Name

Website URL

Username 👤

Password 🔒

Password Hint

Notes

Website Name

Website URL

Username 👤

Password 🔒

Password Hint

Notes

Special Instructions

Website Name

Website URL

Username

Password

Password Hint

Notes

Website Name

Website URL

Username

Password

Password Hint

Notes

Special Instructions

D

Website Name

Website URL

Username 👤

Password 🔒

Password Hint

Notes

Website Name

Website URL

Username 👤

Password 🔒

Password Hint

Notes

Special Instructions

Website Name

Website URL

Username 👤

Password 🔒

Password Hint

Notes

Website Name

Website URL

Username 👤

Password 🔒

Password Hint

Notes

Special Instructions

D

Website Name

Website URL

Username 👤

Password 🔒

Password Hint

Notes

___

Website Name

Website URL

Username 👤

Password 🔒

Password Hint

Notes

___

Special Instructions

Website Name

D

Website URL

Username 👤

Password 🔒

Password Hint

Notes

_____

Website Name

Website URL

Username 👤

Password 🔒

Password Hint

Notes

_____

Special Instructions

E Website Name

Website URL

Username

Password

Password Hint

Notes

Website Name

Website URL

Username

Password

Password Hint

Notes

Special Instructions

Website Name

Website URL

Username

Password

Password Hint

Notes

Website Name

Website URL

Username

Password

Password Hint

Notes

Special Instructions

E

Website Name

Website URL

Username

Password

Password Hint

Notes

Website Name

Website URL

Username

Password

Password Hint

Notes

Special Instructions

Website Name

Website URL

Username 👤

Password 🔒

Password Hint

Notes

Website Name

Website URL

Username 👤

Password 🔒

Password Hint

Notes

Special Instructions

F

Website Name

Website URL

Username 👤

Password 🔒

Password Hint

Notes

Website Name

Website URL

Username 👤

Password 🔒

Password Hint

Notes

Special Instructions

Website Name

Website URL

Username

Password

Password Hint

Notes

Website Name

Website URL

Username

Password

Password Hint

Notes

Special Instructions

F Website Name

Website URL

 Username

Password 🔒

Password Hint

 Notes

Website Name

Website URL

 Username

Password

Password Hint

Notes

Special Instructions

Website Name

Website URL

Username 👤

Password 🔒

Password Hint

Notes

Website Name

Website URL

Username 👤

Password 🔒

Password Hint

Notes

Special Instructions

G Website Name

Website URL

Username 👤

Password 🔒

Password Hint

Notes

Website Name

Website URL

Username 👤

Password 🔒

Password Hint

Notes

Special Instructions

Website Name

Website URL

Username 👤

Password 🔒

Password Hint

Notes

Website Name

Website URL

Username 👤

Password 🔒

Password Hint

Notes

Special Instructions

G Website Name

 Website URL

Username

 Password

Password Hint

 Notes

 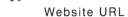

Website Name

Website URL

Username

Password

 Password Hint

Notes

Special Instructions

Website Name

Website URL

Username 👤

Password 🔒

Password Hint

Notes

Website Name

Website URL

Username 👤

Password 🔒

Password Hint

Notes

Special Instructions

H

Website Name

Website URL

Username 👤

Password 🔒

Password Hint

Notes

Website Name

Website URL

Username 👤

Password 🔒

Password Hint

Notes

Special Instructions

Website Name

Website URL

Username

Password

Password Hint

Notes

Website Name

Website URL

Username

Password

Password Hint

Notes

Special Instructions

H Website Name

Website URL

Username

Password

Password Hint

Notes

Website Name

Website URL

Username

Password

Password Hint

Notes

Special Instructions

Website Name

Website URL

Username 👤

Password 🔒

Password Hint

Notes

Website Name

Website URL

Username 👤

Password 🔒

Password Hint

Notes

Special Instructions

Website Name

Website URL

Username 👤

Password 🔒

Password Hint

Notes

Website Name

Website URL

Username 👤

Password 🔒

Password Hint

Notes

Special Instructions

Website Name

Website URL

Username 👤

Password 🔒

Password Hint

Notes

Website Name

Website URL

Username 👤

Password 🔒

Password Hint

Notes

Special Instructions

Website Name

Website URL

Username 👤

Password 🔒

Password Hint

Notes

Website Name

Website URL

Username 👤

Password 🔒

Password Hint

Notes

Special Instructions

Website Name

Website URL

Username

Password

Password Hint

Notes

Website Name

Website URL

Username

Password

Password Hint

Notes

Special Instructions

J Website Name

 Website URL

Username

 Password

Password Hint

 Notes

Website Name

Website URL

Username

Password

 Password Hint

Notes

Special Instructions

Website Name

Website URL

Username

Password

Password Hint

Notes

Website Name

Website URL

Username

Password

Password Hint

Notes

Special Instructions

J Website Name

 Website URL

Username

 Password

Password Hint

 Notes

 Website Name

Website URL

Username

Password

 Password Hint

Notes

Special Instructions

Website Name

Website URL

Username

Password

Password Hint

Notes

Website Name

Website URL

Username

Password

Password Hint

Notes

Special Instructions

K Website Name

 Website URL

Username

 Password 🔒

Password Hint

 Notes

 Website Name

Website URL

Username

 Password

Password Hint

Notes

Special Instructions

Website Name

Website URL

Username 👤

Password 🔒

Password Hint

Notes

Website Name

Website URL

Username 👤

Password 🔒

Password Hint

Notes

Special Instructions

K Website Name

 Website URL

Username

 Password 🔓

Password Hint

 Notes

 Website Name

Website URL

Username

 Password

Password Hint

 Notes

Special Instructions

Website Name

Website URL

Username 👤

Password 🔒

Password Hint

Notes

Website Name

Website URL

Username 👤

Password 🔒

Password Hint

Notes

Special Instructions

L

Website Name

Website URL

Username

Password 🔒

Password Hint

Notes

Website Name

Website URL

Username 👤

Password 🔒

Password Hint

Notes

Special Instructions

Website Name

Website URL

Username

Password

Password Hint

Notes

Website Name

Website URL

Username

Password

Password Hint

Notes

Special Instructions

L

Website Name

Website URL

Username 👤

Password 🔒

Password Hint

Notes

Website Name

Website URL

Username 👤

Password 🔒

Password Hint

Notes

Special Instructions

Website Name

Website URL

Username

Password

Password Hint

Notes

Website Name

Website URL

Username

Password

Password Hint

Notes

Special Instructions

M Website Name

 Website URL

Username

 Password 🔓

Password Hint

 Notes

 Website Name

Website URL

Username

 Password

 Password Hint

Notes

Special Instructions

Website Name

Website URL

Username 👤

Password 🔒

Password Hint

Notes

_____

Website Name

Website URL

Username 👤

Password 🔒

Password Hint

Notes

_____

Special Instructions

Website Name

 Website URL

Username

 Password

Password Hint

 Notes

 Website Name

Website URL

 Username

Password

 Password Hint

Notes

Special Instructions

Website Name

Website URL

Username 👤

Password 🔒

Password Hint

Notes

Website Name

Website URL

Username 👤

Password 🔒

Password Hint

Notes

Special Instructions

Website Name

 Website URL

Username

 Password

Password Hint

 Notes

 Website Name

Website URL

Username

Password

 Password Hint

Notes

Special Instructions

Website Name

Website URL

Username 👤

Password 🔒

Password Hint

Notes

Website Name

Website URL

Username 👤

Password 🔒

Password Hint

Notes

Special Instructions

Website Name

Website URL

Username

Password

Password Hint

Notes

___

Website Name

Website URL

Username

Password

Password Hint

Notes

___

Special Instructions

Website Name

Website URL

Username

Password

Password Hint

Notes

Website Name

Website URL

Username

Password

Password Hint

Notes

Special Instructions

Website Name

Website URL

Username 👤

Password 🔒

Password Hint

Notes

Website Name

Website URL

Username 👤

Password 🔒

Password Hint

Notes

Special Instructions

Website Name

Website URL

Username 👤

Password 🔒

Password Hint

Notes

Website Name

Website URL

Username 👤

Password 🔒

Password Hint

Notes

Special Instructions

Website Name

Website URL

Username 👤

Password 🔒

Password Hint

Notes

Website Name

Website URL

Username 👤

Password 🔒

Password Hint

Notes

Special Instructions

Website Name

Website URL

Username 👤

Password 🔒

Password Hint

Notes

Website Name

Website URL

Username 👤

Password 🔒

Password Hint

Notes

Special Instructions

P Website Name

Website URL

Username 👤

Password 🔒

Password Hint

Notes

Website Name

Website URL

Username 👤

Password 🔒

Password Hint

Notes

Special Instructions

Website Name

Website URL

Username 👤

Password 🔒

Password Hint

Notes

Website Name

Website URL

Username 👤

Password 🔒

Password Hint

Notes

Special Instructions

Website Name

Website URL

Username 👤

Password 🔒

Password Hint

Notes

Website Name

Website URL

Username 👤

Password 🔒

Password Hint

Notes

Special Instructions

Website Name

Website URL

Username 👤

Password 🔒

Password Hint

Notes

Website Name

Website URL

Username 👤

Password 🔒

Password Hint

Notes

Special Instructions

Q Website Name

Website URL

Username 👤

Password 🔒

Password Hint

Notes

Website Name

Website URL

Username 👤

Password 🔒

Password Hint

Notes

Special Instructions

Website Name

Website URL

Username

Password

Password Hint

Notes

Website Name

Website URL

Username

Password

Password Hint

Notes

Special Instructions

Website Name

 Website URL

Username

 Password 🔒

Password Hint

 Notes

 Website Name

Website URL

 Username 👤

Password 🔒

 Password Hint

Notes

Special Instructions

Website Name

Website URL

Username

Password

Password Hint

Notes

Website Name

Website URL

Username

Password

Password Hint

Notes

Special Instructions

R Website Name

 Website URL

Username

 Password

Password Hint

 Notes

 Website Name

Website URL

 Username

Password

 Password Hint

Notes

Special Instructions

Website Name

R

Website URL

Username 👤

Password 🔒

Password Hint

Notes

Website Name

Website URL

Username 👤

Password 🔒

Password Hint

Notes

Special Instructions

R

Website Name
_____

Website URL
_____

Username
_____

Password
_____

Password Hint
_____

Notes
_____

_____

_____

Website Name
_____

Website URL
_____

Username
_____

Password
_____

Password Hint
_____

Notes
_____

_____

_____

Special Instructions

Website Name

Website URL

Username 👤

Password 🔒

Password Hint

Notes

Website Name

Website URL

Username 👤

Password 🔒

Password Hint

Notes

Special Instructions

S

Website Name

 Website URL

Username

 Password

Password Hint

 Notes

Website Name

Website URL

 Username

Password

 Password Hint

Notes

Special Instructions

Website Name

Website URL

Username

Password

Password Hint

Notes

Website Name

Website URL

Username

Password

Password Hint

Notes

Special Instructions

S Website Name

 Website URL

Username

 Password

Password Hint

 Notes

 Website Name

Website URL

Username

 Password

Password Hint

 Notes

Special Instructions

Website Name

Website URL

Username 👤

Password 🔒

Password Hint

Notes

Website Name

Website URL

Username 👤

Password 🔒

Password Hint

Notes

Special Instructions

Website Name

Website URL

Username

Password

Password Hint

Notes

Website Name

Website URL

Username

Password

Password Hint

Notes

Special Instructions

Website Name

Website URL

Username 👤

Password 🔒

Password Hint

Notes

_____

Website Name

Website URL

Username 👤

Password 🔒

Password Hint

Notes

_____

Special Instructions

Website Name

 Website URL

Username

 Password 🔒

Password Hint

 Notes

 Website Name

Website URL

 Username 👤

Password 🔒

 Password Hint

Notes

Special Instructions

Website Name

Website URL

Username 👤

Password 🔒

Password Hint

Notes

Website Name

Website URL

Username 👤

Password 🔒

Password Hint

Notes

Special Instructions

Website Name

 Website URL

Username

 Password 🔒

Password Hint

 Notes

 Website Name

Website URL

Username

 Password 🔒

 Password Hint

Notes

Special Instructions

Website Name

Website URL

Username 👤

Password 🔒

Password Hint

Notes

Website Name

Website URL

Username 👤

Password 🔒

Password Hint

Notes

Special Instructions

Website Name

Website URL

Username

Password

Password Hint

Notes

Website Name

Website URL

Username

Password

Password Hint

Notes

Special Instructions

Website Name

Website URL

Username 👤

Password 🔒

Password Hint

Notes

Website Name

Website URL

Username 👤

Password 🔒

Password Hint

Notes

Special Instructions

Website Name

 Website URL

Username

 Password

Password Hint

 Notes

Website Name

 Website URL

Username

 Password

Password Hint

 Notes

Special Instructions

W

Website Name

Website URL

Username

Password

Password Hint

Notes

Website Name

Website URL

Username

Password

Password Hint

Notes

Special Instructions

X Website Name

 Website URL

Username

 Password 🔒

Password Hint

 Notes

Website Name

 Website URL

Username

Password 🔒

 Password Hint

Notes

Special Instructions

Website Name

Website URL

Username

Password

Password Hint

Notes

Website Name

Website URL

Username

Password

Password Hint

Notes

Special Instructions

Y

Website Name

Website URL

Username

Password

Password Hint

Notes

Website Name

Website URL

Username

Password

Password Hint

Notes

Special Instructions

Website Name

Website URL

Username 👤

Password 🔒

Password Hint

Notes

_____

Website Name

Website URL

Username 👤

Password 🔒

Password Hint

Notes

_____

Special Instructions

Z

Website Name

 Website URL

Username

 Password

Password Hint

 Notes

Website Name

 Website URL

Username

Password

 Password Hint

Notes

Special Instructions

Website Name

Website URL

Username

Password

Password Hint

Notes

Website Name

Website URL

Username

Password

Password Hint

Notes

Special Instructions

Miscellaneous

Website Name

Website URL

Username 👤

Password 🔒

Password Hint

Notes

Website Name

Website URL

Username 👤

Password 🔒

Password Hint

Notes

🐾 🐾 🐾 🐾 🐾 🐾 🐾 🐾 🐾

Miscellaneous

Website Name

Website URL

Username

Password

Password Hint

Notes

Website Name

Website URL

Username

Password

Password Hint

Notes

Account

Username

Password

Password Hint

Notes

___

Account

Username

Password

Password Hint

Notes

___

Special Instructions

Account

Username

Password

Password Hint

Notes

Account

Username

Password

Password Hint

Notes

Special Instructions

RESOURCES

IDEAS & NOTES

www.ingramcontent.com/pod-product-compliance
Lightning Source LLC
Chambersburg PA
CBHW071007050326
40689CB00014B/3526